THE STORIES OF MY LIFE

Books by Michael Schmidt

POETRY
New and Collected Poems, Sheep Meadow, 2010
Collected Poems, smith|doorstop, 2009
The Resurrection of the Body, smith|doorstop, 2006, Sheep Meadow, 2007
Selected Poems, smith|doorstop, 1997
The Love of Strangers, Century Hutchinson, 1989
Choosing a Guest: New and Selected Poems, Anvil, 1983

LITERARY HISTORY AND CRITICISM
The Novel: a Biography, Harvard University Press, 2014
The Story of Poetry I-III, Weidenfeld, 2001-2008
Lives of the Ancient Poets: The Greeks, Weidenfeld, 2004, Knopf, 2005
Lives of the Poets, Weidenfeld, 1998, Knopf, 1999
Reading Modern Poetry, Routledge, 1989
Fifty Modern British Poets: an introduction, Pan/Heinemann, 1979
Fifty English Poets 1300-1900: an introduction, Pan/Heinemann, 1979

NOVELS
The Dresden Gate, Century Hutchinson, 1988
The Colonist, Muller/Hutchinson, 1983

TRANSLATIONS
On Poets & Others, Octavio Paz, Paladin, 1991
Flower & Song: Nahuatl Poetry (with Edward Kissam), Anvil, 1977

POETRY ANTHOLOGIES
New Poetries I-V, Carcanet, 1994-2011
Four American Poets, Carcanet, 2010
The Great Modern Poets, Quercus, 2007
The Harvill Book of Twentieth-Century Poetry in English, Harvill, 1999

THE STORIES OF MY LIFE

MICHAEL SCHMIDT

Sheep Meadow Press
Rhinebeck, NY

Designed and typeset by The Sheep Meadow Press
Distributed by The University Press of New England

Cover image: Dosso Dossi, *Jupiter, Mercury and Virtue*

Library of Congress Cataloging-in-Publication Data

Names: Schmidt, Michael, 1947- author.
Title: The stories of my life / Michael Schmidt.
Description: Rhinebeck, NY : Sheep Meadow Press, 2016.
Identifiers: LCCN 2015044756 | ISBN 9781937679583
Classification: LCC PR6069.C52 A6 2016 | DDC 821/.914--dc23
LC record available at http://lccn.loc.gov/2015044756

All inquiries and permission requests should be addressed to the publisher:

The Sheep Meadow Press
PO Box 84
Rhinebeck, NY 12514

There was the Long Room, at one end of the garden, at the other the great gilded mirror,
all blotches and dimples and ripples. I fluctuated in the watery glass; according to the light
I retreated into the depths of the aquarium, or trembled in the foreground like a thread of
pale-green samphire. Those who thought they knew me were ignorant of the creature I scarcely
knew myself.

  —Patrick White
  Flaws in the Glass: A Self-Portrait

But perhaps the time has come to give a name to the image appearing in the mirror's depth,
which the painter in front of the picture contemplates.

  —Michel Foucault
  "Las Meninas," part II, *les mots et les choses*

Acknowledgments

Versions of some of these poems appeared in *The First Poets* (Knopf), *The Word Exchange* (W.W. Norton, 2010), *The Palm Beach Effect: Reflections on Michael Hofmann* (CB Editions, 2013), *Soul Feathers*, for Macmillan Cancer Support (2011), *Of Love and Hope*, a poetry anthology in aid of Breakthrough Breast Cancer and Breast Cancer Care (2010), and in *Oxford Magazine, PN Review, Poetry, Parnassus, Stand, The Reader* and *Tri-Quarterly*. The Greville Press pamphlet *Family Tree* was published in 2010, and for that I owe thanks to Anthony Astbury, one of poetry's champions. Four poems here were published in the "new poems" section of my *Collected Poems* (2010).

"The Education of Henry Adams" was commissioned for *Lines in Long Array: a Civil War Commemoration* edited by David C. Ward and Frank H. Goodyear III and published by the Smithsonian, National Portrait Gallery, Washington D.C. (2013).

Many of the poems in this book were published in the United Kingdom by Smith Doorstop Ltd.

The publisher thought that the reader would like very much to have a few of Schmidt's earlier poems, that inform some of the later poems included in this book, conveniently at hand. We are most grateful to various of his other publishers for not howling their objections.

for my cousin Joan McAllister

CONTENTS

ARCHEOLOGY

DIVINE POEMS

TWICE-TOLD TALES

For My Father

I learn the dead wear shoes.
Their beards cast a last shadow.
Kissing your face,
I'm troubled by the roughness
As when you came to tuck me up,
Brushed my cheek with yours
And tip-toed out.

Scorpion
for John Schmidt

Under its stone, it pleats and unpleats ebony,
it digs a bed which is a body-print exactly,
room for pincer, tail and sting.
If it elbows out, it leaves
cold evidence of tenancy.

Bedded with it, less precise,
ambling grubs and sloe-worms
eat and burrow deep sometimes as earthworms,
not worrying that fast eel of their element—
it flinches, deadly at a grain's shift.

I follow you hunting with jar and trowel.
Each time you turn the right stone up:
warm flat stones which roof an airless square of dark
and hold all night the sun's warmth
for the black king-pin of the poor soil.

The stone raised, the creature's tense and cocked.
Tail curled, it edges forward, backward—its enemy
so big he is invisible (though a child)
hunched over it, who trembles too
at such a minute potency.

And you flick it with the trowel into the jar.
It jerks and flings its fire in all directions
at hard transparency. You bear it to an anthill,
tip it on the dust. Like a cat it drops
right side up, into a red tide of pincers.

It twitches its tail and twice stings itself—
to death. Piece by piece it is removed
underground by the ants—a sort of burial—
perhaps to be reassembled as an effigy
somewhere deeper than we can know

bound home with an empty jar,
the field full of upturned stones.

Wasps' Nest

It was the fruit I wanted, not the nest.
The nest was hanging like the richest fruit
against the sun. I took the nest

and with it came the heart, and in my hand
the kingdom and the queen, frail surfaces,
rested for a moment. Then the drones

awoke and did their painful business.
I let the city drop upon the stones.
It split to its deep palaces and combs.

It bled the insect gold,
the pupa queens like tiny eyes
wriggled from their sockets, and somewhere

the monarch cowered in a veil of wings
in passages through which at evening
the labourers had homed,

burdened with silence and the garden scents.
The secret heart was broken suddenly.
I, to whom the knowledge had been given,

who was not after knowledge but a fruit,
remember how a knot of pains
swelled my hand to a round nest;

blood throbbed in the hurt veins
as if an unseen swarm mined there.
The nest oozed bitter honey.

I swaddled my fat hand in cotton.
After a week pain gave it back to me
scarred and weakened like a shrivelled skin.

A second fruit is growing on the tree.
Identical—the droning in the leaves.
It ripens. I have another hand.

The Freeze

We can't sleep tonight. The ice has formed—
from thin skin at evening
to deep stone. With midnight
the boat's aground in it.
Planks shriek against the hardening.

Below deck a film of frost pales everything.
Our breath makes beads of ice. We pace
between the hatch and bunks.
The world would end by ice
tonight, for sure, if we lay down.

Come outside: the wind has sculpted
sails to marble drapery; on the line
our laundry freezes to a rigor-mortis.
Night will hardly darken all this glass—
the stars are treble on its rippled plane.

We started from a tropic on whose shore
the lizards' tongues were flames of malachite
in leaves that trailed on to the tide,
and crimson fish were couriers there
to caverns where eels uncoiled their sting.

Night plankton burned our wake—
for years we have been heading north.
When lips are tucked away for good
and rigid as ice-starched shirt and trousers
we pass the climax of our slow miasma,

and the river hardens in the arteries
till the heart with the hull surrenders
to stillness and is broken like a stone,
when our histories are minuted, adjourned,
our faces upturned to a Sabbath star,

this will be the scene if we can see,
the fish arrested with the drifting tires,
the dry snow driven into dunes of ash.
It was not like this in the other place—
there all was fire and water,

nothing stilled the waves
that might be furious though they never died
to the intolerable vacancy
we pace to keep the blood awake. Come down.
We'll light the burner, thaw our fingers out.

We are the ashes that will cover us,
our inch of life, our mile, our field of breathing.

Augustine

Now I have seen the man
      The Manichee I was
Withdraws to the phantom cross
      And hangs in darkness there.

Some part of me is damned
      For ever. Let it go.
The fire will deal with it
      As quickly as a leaf.

I spare that little ash
      And turn to the real flesh.
A man with angel's eyes
      Stands by me with the nails.

He whispers that the beams
      With bark as thick as skin
Will hold my body firm
      As they have held before

Even a man like him
      Who looked with angel's eyes.
I take from his broken hand
      The spikes of paradise.

"Until I Built the Wall"

Until I built the wall they did not find me.
Sweet anarchy! attending quietly
To wild birds or picking the blackberry.

Trespassers did not know they erred and came
In and away, leaving the land the same.
The hunter went to richer ground for game.

Tending, profitless, my property
Which no map mentioned, where no metal lay
In veins beneath the surface of hard clay

And bristle grass, I watched my livestock—scores
Of lizards, armadillos, and the birds—
Free citizens. I had concealed no snares.

Mere ground. Mere nothing harvested or sown.
But how the shadows made the rough design
Live as a landscape for the man alone!

So I grew proud. That's why I built the wall
Of stone and mortar, and I drove a nail
Into a stake and hung a sign to tell

The wanderer *Private Land*, with guarantees
Of instant death for *anyone who tries*
To enter here: leave hope. Vain promises!

Who would I kill or could I kill?
Before I turned a servant of the will
To mark my ground, indeed, who would I hurt or kill?

Now peering from the rim of my high wall
I see the plain outside abruptly shrill
With enemies I do not know. They call

Who's in there, what do you mean, and why?
I hold my peace, but they've discovered me
Because I drew a line, a *Here am I.*

They rob my peace, they take away my sleep.
Their voices drizzle all the night. I step
Along the wall as round a castle keep

Till in the daylight there they stand again,
Drawn up from their shadows till at noon
Ghost warriors hover by the place I own.

As ribs around a heart, the gentle wall
Tucks in the land, or as a crisp snail shell
Cups its soft cause. Yet yearlong vigil

Sours memory of the lovely ground,
Rivets to masonry the heart and hand:
I tend a straitened altitude of stone.

Choice

I am like the worm.
Cut in two, I'd thrive.
Within the metaphor
I greet myself, I take
My right hand in my right
And looking eye to eye
I'm satisfied. I need
A knife to make it true,
A simple slice, and clean;
Another lover too.

The worm resembles me.
The rough dark hardens it.
Within the metaphor
It only knows it is
And not which way it goes
To what, from what, how far.
I want a blade to fall
Between me so I move
Forward fore and aft
And double the odds for love.

The worm and I emerge
Into the rainy light.
We wander on the lawn
And lose our entrances.
I kneel on a flagstone
And press it with my thumb.
It twists into a ring
And writhes away again.
Here resemblance ends
Like casual marriages.

Piano

You can make music come from those cold keys.
Alone and grandly I adjust the stool,
Flap up my shirt tail, take your seat, arrange
Feet on the pedals, poise my hands, then pause.
Around me evening holds its breath.

Accustomed as I am to hear you play,
I hear you with my hands above the keys
And can imagine that I sit apart
Patient, watching your shoulders move
Into the music as a dancer sways,

Your intimacy with a sheet of notes
I can't approach, your feet that press
Gently the brass pedals so they take
A chord as far as you would have it go
Or clear the air of music instantly.

There, your sleeves turned
Up to the elbow, and your forearms pale
Above the ivory and the shadow keys
On evenings like this . . . the ghost of you
Compels me to keep silence in your place.

Here and There

There, you are climbing to the Aber Falls.
Here, at my table, I think of you:
The mist around you and your body's pulse
Makes its own intimate atmosphere
From which you gaze out loving that landscape—
You pass the wild horses and the marsh trees.
Here, beside myself, I follow you.

Last year we went that path in rain and found
The falls come out of cloud, not off a cliff:
A torrent poured by the invisible. We took
Shoes and socks off, waded to the pool.
Slipping, letting go, who cares; in deep
Up to the waist, with the fish, we moved
Under the fall's full weight.
The water struck us like an avalanche.

The weather never cleared. It won't today.
There, now, you may have reached the upper pool.
You may be taking off your shoes and socks.
Here, I flex my toes inside my shoes.
Shall I go take a bath? I ask you:
How to wash this image out, erase
Trees, the hand in hand, the shaft of water,
Its force that knocked me dumb into your arms?

The Honeysuckle

Your honeysuckle, since you've been away
Breathes heavily. Your room is full of scent.
I look into the dusk. Your labour's there,
The tending that gradually seduced
Soil and stem to render up a pattern.
Your work becomes like theirs, as they reduce
Their straggling to ordered scent and hue,
Hospitable to birds. Your only care
Is measuring of growth, decay; and time
Is seasons of the bud, the withering,
Unabstract, with unspoken promises.

Unbroken, too. Each year the place prepares,
Punished and loved—two passions of one heart—
To give what profit a beloved can give.
You choose that time of year to go,
Leaving to me the climax. I'm not in love
With greenery, but you—and left with what you made
Of a small garden and a broken tree
I fumble with your chores, meek but unbeguiled.

Evening takes off the brilliance by degrees
Until the poppy is a ghost, the rose
A bruise among its foliage; then dark
Fills in the scented trough between the hedges,
Extinguishes the tree, absolves the eye from all
Reality. I lie in your dark room
Intent to think of nothing, sleep.
Only, the honeysuckle comes,
An air that you prepared, to fill your place.

From The Love of Strangers

. . . something remains apart from what you spoke of,
Something that's mine, I can't be sure of it.
                                 Who showed me—it was you—
The great black rose window in some chapel—
And the Sequoiahs, did I go down on my knees?
And here below, a sad, a shadowy house . . . and who is she?
I came—I must have come—full of love and my cot
Was cold, the room was cold. There were bears and creatures.
Days passed, you were the long hand of the clock
Morning and evening, morning and evening, time went by
With its feasts, its toys and solstices, till rose
And cold room were memory and less than that,
An almost deadened nerve; but the gilded cornices,
The steep sash, the sickles of the trees come back
Now that I have a son. How cold is his room?

I am standing tall myself
As a grandfather clock.
                              If it were not for time
We could be brothers, the three of us.
As it is I feel your cheekbones in my smile,
Your gestures bend my arms and wag my head.
The pure tone of your whistle finds my lips
As if I was an echo, a reflection,
And you stood over there with your neutral smile
Watching what time, not silvered glass,
Does to the very last of your sloughed skins.

Half of my life you've been dead
And yet not absent for a single day! I steer continually
By your prohibitions. "Dear Papacito," school letters began
When most of the time I meant to wound. After all,
You'd sent me four thousand miles into exile
And called it education. I had grievances. I hurt you

Because you were too guileless not to trust me.
You wadded up draft after draft of your replies
But kept my letters in a drawer
In your steel roll-top desk at Pino 458.
After you died I found them stashed there
As if they were love letters. But this is the first.

III

One by one your friends
Fell to the force of sensible arrangements,
Sowed themselves in prosperous soil and grew
their various houses. In the high windows
Children's faces showed, and they came down.
We aged, our taproots deep in compromise
And money. We have become a benign forest now,
A little jealous of your liberty.
We patronize you as we do the memory of our own youth,
As though you were a child
Who touched in us a silted innocence.

Free spirit! Free within this loving forest
Where you are home a few more easy years,
If there were a room here large enough
It would be yours for ever, as we are.
But can you settle with those words that are
Air and your air, and on that countryscape
Whose shapes conceal the lover that you seek?

IV

. . . I've never known
A man so worldly, the right books on his shelves
If he could only lay his hands on them,
Cursory, eclectic, his optimism
Naive jetsam of a precocious childhood. By running on before,

Then running back with stale "I told you so's,"
A sort of prophet after the event, he passed as wise for a time.

In retrospect he must have drawn a hundred times the map
That leads to his blank bed, his faded page.
On principle he avoided the War but it took everything;
His history stopped at 1938—*annus mirabilis*, the novel,
The great success that History swallowed.
                                                                    A man so eager
To catch the boat, and the boat pulling away, leaving him
With his trunk and hopes on the quay! He amazed me the first time
With his urbanity. Later he trotted out the same anecdotes
Like a soldier who chews your ear with one old battle.
Each time I went to his tall gilded flat he had
Something urgent to show me he just couldn't find
On those sagging shelves of literature, and evening
Folded us into dim armchairs, whiskies in our hands and him
Still talking, unwilling to let go . . .

            V

If he'd been a bird he would have had no feathers:
Sharp beak, sharp talons, a voice pure as water
Just at freezing point, or the mind at sleep
On the point of transformation.
                                                    His last book's inscribed
Plein d'amitié—Janos Pilinsky; the first was fuller:
Plein de remerciments et d'amitié: du sollst mich nicht
Vergessen. That's how we talked in Babel, trading phrases,
The small change of language. Yet he meant it.

I tease out an image of yours: how she wipes the mirror,
For it strikes her that the frame is beautiful;
The glass should be worthy of it, of the room.
She polishes the dust away, the cobwebs,
Stands back and is rewarded by—herself.

Aproned, red-faced, her hairy arms and lip.
"At least the job is done." "At least it's true,
The thing she sees." "It's not the thing she sought."
"She was not seeking, really. Was she seeking?"
"Not really, but like Picasso said, she found;
Like Saint Teresa, she found it in the stew,
In menial circumstance, in dailiness. She looked
And was dazed by the visual irony—
The gilt about her! The carved fruit and leaves
Framing the least servant, I forget her name."
As if a murderer found he wore a halo
And was borne by an archangel at each hand.

You were borne by angels till they dropped you:
The army of heaven has become so clumsy.
You are dead now and I don't forget you,
Or how you startled yourself, incongruous
But real in the frame of every poem.
You were after gravity, and earth,
But found the rags of spirit on the wire,
And found the wire, too, and the flanking trench.

    VI

        . . . Why can't I put out of mind
Those coiling gourds of his last prison period,
Those gourds that twist on their rough dish
And rise, as if they grew
From that captivity into the world
His revolution has not made?
And there were zinnias, white fire, walls
Falling, rifles, bones; he grew
Into himself in prison, like Genet,
Holding a brush in one hand and his hard
Penis in the other, not for love:
Art of a damaged son, child of a damaged land

Pygmalion, making a thing he must control,
Praying History to put colour in its cheeks.
When it steps free of the easel will it speak
From his own lips? Muddying his palette
With rage and desperation, his changing heart
Was never in this world.
                              Architect of clouds.

   VIII

. . . The editor handed back my review:
Why write peasant Spanish,
A man like you, with your education?
Send it to me in English. I'll get it translated
By someone who sins less against the language.

If I could introduce him to my teacher!
I have only her to blame,
Her and her village—Cuacalco, under the squat hill.
One time she took me to see where she grew up—
Without a father, I later deduced; where she bore
Her one child without a husband, left him
To an aunt when my father gave her work.
And how she worked! Dark mother, dark grandmother,
Fed me, kept me clean, let me ride on her back,
Taught me her language, told me her story
Time after time, always the same words,
Yet the same words real as though she'd just found them.
I was the stand-in for her dismal baby,
She called me *hijo*; last time I visited
She took for granted I was her only son . . .

IX

. . . Aloof from the *blind nurses of racial character*
You evolved a mystic disregard for commerce,
For war, assassination; instead adhered
To what does not change, is not destroyed,
What you share with Sumer, Greece and Alexandria,
With Amherst, Weimar. Hampton Court,
Curious territory no single map contains,
A Geist without race, which cannot be annexed,
Enjoined, perverted, a refinement
Hungry for forms and the few sharp timeless truths.

The *barren severities* of history, Persia taught you,
Made no lasting wound on a real culture,
Any more than the adjustments of an intellectual border
Affected the capital of human sense—
As if Darwin, Marx and Freud had not clouded the sky
With their unsettling breath; how long have they lived
Compared with Homer? What is their style,
Have they really touched language or only words?
Would this plane, this beech
This cypress tree survive in Eden or Utopia,
Or only here?
                    The mind is a garden, as the garden is
And hangs above a wilderness it comprehends.
To lose sight, to see the garden fade out gradually,
Not because it changes, but we change,
Brings round the last term of old wisdom, death,
Clean of fear and superstition.
The tiny islands of pleasure, the reefs where love ran aground
Are lost, each private temple falls, and yet,
As you knew they would, the week you died
The flowers kept their scent,
And not a word you wrote became less true.

XIV

. . . You fled west with the human flood of disaffection,
Settled in Kansas, then Colorado, down the map
To Mexico, then south, then further south ...
Dogged still by history—Prussia, Pancho Villa,
Liquidators, conscience: almost prosperous
Time after time, shopkeeper, impresario, clerk;
Almost destitute.
                        Failure's hero, you could not acknowledge
The huge vindictive goddess riding her storm cloud
Behind your little billowing wake of dust
Down the spine of both Americas
Until your final venture failed in Chile.

Five decades of declining years
Under the kind, unjudging care of my aunts,
And the President of the United States himself,
The Irish one, *und auch Papistisch,*
Wished you a happy century.
And even that was not the end of it
At Mar Vista, your dogs, hours on the porch just swinging
On the plaid garden seat. I was presented to
Old ladies you were allowed to court.
There was your case of rusty books, the regimented
Gothic tombstones of your complete, uncut Goethe,
And you subsiding into German . . .

XV

It wasn't snowing but it should have been.
You were an old man, nine months from the grave.
Your hand was very dry and very hot
And large, as I recall (I was a boy,
Fourteen years at most, I led you round
Part of the school, your guide; you seemed to listen).
That night you read in a slow, dismissive voice

That left the words like notes on staves hung in the air,
No longer yours, but part of memory—
You talked about Miss Dickinson of Amherst
And said aloud the eight lines of her poem
'The heart asks pleasure first'. And from that night
I've known the poem word-perfect, part of me.

I think you let more lines free into language
And memory with your rusty, lonely voice
Than any other poet of our age.
It must have been like freeing doves
And watching them go off to neighbouring cotes
Or into the low clouds of your New Hampshire
Knowing they'll meet no harm, that they'll survive
Long after the hand that freed them has decayed.

Those lines are wise in rhythm and they lead
Into a clapboard dwelling, or a field,
Or lives that prey upon the land and one another,
Or the big country where we both were children.

XVII

. . . He translated Greek badly, Latin badly;
The Aztec he rendered as though
The nineteenth century had dawned yesterday
In all its brutal freshness on the heart.
But he knew the Aztec language perfectly from books
Having transcribed the chronicles, annotated
The sacred hymns, the prayers, the chants of war;
He was Sahagún and every lesser witness,
Ghosting the figures buried in the silt
Of histories that History had displaced.

I'd not imagined rooms
So dusty, cold, so inhospitable,

Rooms like a dictionary, without waste
Or scruple, good manners or good cheer.
Then he appeared before me and I rose
Too quickly for politeness, more like fear.
His arms hugged his chest, as if he was cold in a shroud,
His hands and face were bleached, his beard, his eyes too seemed
All whites. I never saw a creature so bloodless,
As though he had strayed out of the past,
Or a cloud, or a grave. 'Don Angel!' I exclaimed,
Unfolded his reluctant hand
And did what the Indians do, I kissed it.
And then I blushed because I wasn't Roman Catholic
Or Christian. For the first time in my life
I smelled on him the stale scent
Of utter solitude and abstinence,
Of a man without vanity of the flesh,
Of Jerome, the smell of the desert,
The lonely scholar and the chaste shepherd.
What were his angels? Angels without wings,
The lame and halt, the kind whose place in heaven
Is guaranteed by the beatitudes . . .

XVIII

. . . That day with *capote* and *muleta*
It had pleased him to dazzle us. It was a tienta
Where they test livestock to see how strong the blood is.
Matadors practise without the need
To kill or count applause, as a virtuoso might
Bow to silence, adjust the stool,
Play his best preludes to an empty room.
He dazzled us all the same, we were hoarse with cheering,
Until an enormous creature with splayed horns
Pinned him against a *burladero*,
Kept butting, butting him for a full minute.

We carried him gently, as though an angel had fallen.
'I'm not hurt,' he said. That he had to say it
Meant he was hurting, but it was his business.
We lay him on a bench in the shade and fanned him.
Then he walked off by himself beyond the stables.

'How are you now?' I asked when he came to bathe.
He showed me on the skin the horns' abrasions,
Two long burns like grill-marks scorched on steak.
'A little to either side and the kidneys might have been
Unhappy tonight,' he said, then he showed me over
Each of the twenty scars on calf, thigh, groin.
It was a map, each gore a history. 'And the worst
Was this one,' a little livid ridge, he winced to see it.
I stared, repelled and choked by love, considering
A body wounded and risen from its ashes
Twenty times, to triumphs I had witnessed . . .

     XX

After twenty years of 'flying visits',
My 'pressing affairs' and 'I can spare about a week',
You're hardly stranger dead than when you lived,
But for this sadness like a fog I can't see through
That will not clear, that rises from your body;
Or a smoke of death, and scentless,
The air of love now visible, milk-white.

If I had heart I'd number all the losses.
It's the real love I wasted. Even when I chose
Exile in resentment it was there. I knew it given
And only death could take it, which it has,
Setting it where it echoes like a call
Morning, evening, now. If I try to walk,
As an infant risks first steps towards coaxing arms,
I fall half way, and take amiss the loving laughter.
Rubbing my eyes I rise and try again.

Third Persons

If only he hadn't answered the door when she knocked,
    The phone when she called,
If when he started to write his most brilliant story
    He'd expunged her arrival,
Choosing instead to introduce an easier lover
    Or, in place of marriage, travel . . .

It's chilling to witness her coming, her hand on the knocker.
    He was older, maybe, settled.
She came with tears and charm and magic perhaps.
    I don't recall. Startled
Into a posture of love, and grateful (she was, after all,
    Young, beautiful),

He embraced her and for a decade, more, let himself believe
    He loved her, even after
Her eyes turned, and her head, in so many obvious directions
    And her laughter
Spread like pink blossom over numerous other lawns,
    Spread deeper and softer,

And blithely she gave herself up to many surprises of love.
    He could not finish it.
He could not close the poisoned chapter. He could not breathe.
    He gave her the benefit
Of every single, every single doubt, resisting, yet at last
    He threw the story out.

"His father was a baker . . ."
for A.G.G.

His father was a baker, he the youngest son.
I understand they beat him, and they loved him.

His father was a baker in Oaxaca:
I understand his bakery was the best

And his three sons and all his daughters helped
As children with the baking and the pigs.

I can imagine chickens in their patio,
At Christmastime a wattled turkey-cock, a dog

Weathered like a wash-board, yellow-eyed,
That no one stroked, but ate the scraps of bread

And yapped to earn his keep. I understand
The family prospered though the father drank

And now the second brother drinks, often
To excess. I understand as well that love

Came early, bladed, and then went away
And came again in other forms, some foreign,

And took him by the heart away from home.
His father was a baker in Oaxaca

And here I smell the loaves that rose in ovens
Throughout a childhood not yet quite complete

And smell the fragrance of his jet-black hair,
Taste his sweet dialect that is mine too,

Until I understand I am to be a baker,
Up before dawn with trays and trays of dough

To feed him this day, next day and for ever—
Or for a time—the honey-coloured loaves.

Entries from the Cactus Garden, Oaxaca

The teddy bear cholla and the fat fat

Oh buckthorn, devil, whipple, teddy bear

Oh beavertail, oh pancake, porcupine

Oh plump saguaro with your hairy arms, I love
Each of you with a different nerve of heart.
Especially you, so trim, so pert, your birds
Cupped in your pits and crotches, little friends

Oh areoles and aureoles, the orioles
With yellow caps are havering and hot
Making themselves a breeze with their cut wings

I ask the docent and he indicates

Oh nation, how you might have been, spread from
So sure an order, with such tendering love

SECULAR POEMS

Agatha

What is it like in heaven, Agatha?
I see you in those tight scuffed shoes, now dangling
Not over the playground wall (and your sharp knees
And the frayed serge skirt of your school uniform)
But off a black cloud hard against the blue.
They swing to and fro, to and fro, what can you see
So high above my head, and the tree and the hill?

Am I down here, is your house, is your lame cat Dorcas
With whiskers on the left side of her face
And a broken tail? Can you see us, do you want to now,
Recalled by the school alarm, the smell of asphalt
Softening in the sun, and the effulgent haze,
Or is all this fading, faded, faded out? If so, if your
Eyes have been able to uproot themselves from us,
Do they feed on the entire firmament, is it blue,
And is this as though it never had been at all,
Where I stand, where you used to sit on the wall?

What is it like, dear skinny Agatha
With your sharp ribs under a stained singlet, your flat
Chest with nipples stuck on like round plasters,
Like valves, like coppers tipped slightly on smooth sand?
(We walked on the level shore at Capistrano
Gathering dark sand dollars and coolie-hat shells;
First we were five and six, then six and seven.)
What is it like, your straight lips pursed, your grey eyes, Agatha,
Gazing at a sky you're new in and new to?

And what is it like, dear Agatha, without me?
What colour is your hair now, how do you wear it?
Still in braids, or piled up high, in a bun or ponytail?
I stand beneath your cloud and ask and ask.

Departure Lounge

In that yell I heard your childhood cry
Out again, a protracted crying.
It made the woman carrying put
The dreadful bundle down and leave it
Squirming on the grass, and stand apart
Breathing deeply by the lake (the swans
Circling) watching the swans. The squirrels
Approach the squalling child and chuckle
Close by its swollen face, their brown eyes
Big, their tails pluming, three squirrels, then four
And your voice in that voice down all those
Years and lawns and lakes. Can I now reach
Your distress and take it in hand, hold
Close at my chest what you were, make some
Kind of peace?
                    Delivering me red-eyed
At the airport at six this morning
You scalded your lips with a bitter
Costa coffee. Just before I left,
For the first time in years you broke, words
Sharp like your cries were back then. I should
Have stayed with you, whatever. They called
My flight, we hugged. "Back in a fortnight,"
I said and put the dreadful bundle
Down, in its need, in pain, by the lake,
Making my way helpless through customs
As she was then, as we are, fathers,
Mothers, when at last the child knows how
To speak his urgency, and we go.
The flight is called. I wave from the gate.

She Said

He went that way, quite fast, under the yellow tree
With a face red as a smacked behind, tears in his eyes,
Wearing again, she said, the moleskin trousers and tartan waistcoat
He wore to her wedding, the first, when the slut first said yes
Meaning the no it took her years to utter.

Oh, she remembered the waistcoat well enough, and she saw
How it became him despite the wake of years.
He was twenty-two again for a moment, she nineteen,
Her hair pulled back tight in a jet-black bun
And they stood there face to face with his hand on her breast.

How much she loved him still, how much she loved him!
It was easier to say no this second time,
Much easier, thanks to the practice she had had,
Thanks to the afternoon, and autumn, and he was old
And her heart had never healed so it didn't break again

When she felt his breath on her nape as he asked her.
That way, under the yellow tree, he went, she said,
In his tartan waistcoat, this time he was really gone
For good, she said, as though it mattered to her.

Feeding the Baby

                    . . . in the end
She fed her vampire everything she had,
Mother and father first, her husband
(In some ways she was glad to see him go);
Then the children one by one by one,
Keeping back, held close under her shawl
Her favourite, in a milky gown, scowling,
Fat-handed, the pinkest mouthful of all.
When there was nothing left, she fed him
That one too, its salty fingers, china eyes,
Watched his slow jaw work a way right through it,
The baby shrilling a song as babies do
While it could, waving its bloody feet.
The vampire licked his chops and looked straight at her.

How much of her was his, was him by now,
Transformed to tissue, then to excrement,
And still he wasn't hers though she presumed
She'd earned herself a husband, he a wife.

She'd got no more to give. The vampire left her
One evening, not moonlit—"just going to the shops . . ."

Carlisle to Kendal

A tumble of hills and then
that enchanted tower by
the river bend sensed even
in the dark, below Carlisle.

In the Woodcutter's Hut

In the woodcutter's hut the mattresses were stuffed
With beech leaves and their scent. The drifting snow
Blacked out the window, sealed the door, we breathed
Thanks to the stone chimney. In fact,
It wasn't really cold, we had the cask,
Salt beef, the crate and loaves.
                              How the hours,
The hours slowed down, the nights, then the week also,
How they slowed
To breathing in the dark, the rise and fall,
And the pulse hardly ticking wrist and temple.

It seemed like days and days, we couldn't count,
We didn't talk in the dark, we didn't touch.
The beech trees told their season rosary,
From spring through autumn, over and over.
                              Cut
Before the sap was out of them, they stayed
Alive and in the blackout
We hibernated and were unafraid
Because the beech leaves kept telling their story
And when we dozed they lived again on our boughs,
In the good air we swayed, the beech leaves turning
First red, then green, then copper, and bright birds
Swam among them, perched, whetted their bills on our knuckles.
We were the beech boughs, tree skeletons, the gracious copse.
How long we slept! How they made use of us!
Without those mattresses we wouldn't have survived.
Now we're mast and nut and foliage, their bough, their tree.

Present Tense

The old man chews the air.
Under the ground his bride
Travels north and south
Transmitted by the worms,
Moles that scrabble through,
Maggot, vole and shrew.
When resurrection comes
Christ will have to raise
An entire field, she'll stand
On trunks for feet and pray
Like Laura turned to tree
With bough and bloom, her grey
Pupils made of dew,
Pulse a stammering breeze.

The old man senses her
And he is in her arms
Again, ago; both young
Exchange like ventricles,
Touch calling, answering touch,
Two climates, hemispheres,
Resolved in storm, in calm.

Under the chestnut's broad
Candled canopy
Clenched and comfortably
Alone he hugs his knees.
Among forget-me-not,
Bluebell and campion
He leans on a bending branch;
A smell of chamomile
Where his two feet are splayed
Rises from scuffed soil.

Then, into her dark leaves
Plump with the year, a flare,
A ring-dove: how she coos
Among the candles, light.
He listens to her voice,
Breathing the scented air.
Almost the scent is taste,
Almost the taste is touch.

His task is less than Christ's:
Her resurrection comes
To him as oxygen,
The voice, the chamomile;
She reaches like a hand
And closes on his heart.
A sweet time, this, to be
Alive and unalone,
Grace immaterial—
Reflection, not reflex.
He chews the given air.
It feeds him like a host.

Desire

Did we feel desire? We felt it. We felt desire.
And what did we do with it? We suffered it
Behind the ribs, between the eyes and the ears,
In bowel and groin, as if struggling for breath,
As if we had been tackled or felled or had fallen
Out of a normal day onto a fist.
Our own palms sweated and pricked,
We peered out between our fingers. It had not seen us.

What did we do next? We read it, we got it by heart;
We put our ears to it and heard its little lungs
Puffing. We kept it warm, we fed it sweet things,
We sang to it, we turned it on its bed,
Plumped its pillow, cleared away the pans.
We held it close, it smelled yeasty, it smelled of soil.
What did we do? For a year we harboured it,
As if we were a modest town by a bay

And it dropped anchor, furled its sails, ran up its pennants . . .
The beautiful sailors with their sharp starched blue flaps,
The captain a wingless angel . . . no, the captain a man,
And at night the Chinese lanterns, bobbing, enchanting,
An ensemble of pipes, tabors and a fiddle
Shuffling the heart, making it dance. It danced.
We watched from the quay and never went aboard.
They urged and urged us but we never went aboard.

One day it was all over. We woke, it had gone.
Like when the circus leaves a suburb lifeless,
Or it's Epiphany and all the lighted trees
Smoulder in back yards and the smoke makes tears.
We turned to one another then with nothing to hold
But one another. We stayed in the town by the bay.
A moon swelled out of the sea and, once risen, abated
Into a now literal night we inhabit together.

The Bus Stop

I missed the bus, and then it was of course
Too late to catch the train.
Rain came down through the shelter roof.
I sucked a cigarette and watched the rain.

I sucked a cigarette and tried to think
What, in the circumstances, I should do.
It was dark. There were lighted windows across the way,
Behind one of which, no doubt, were you,

Which is why I was in the cold and also why
I got there too late for the bus, and then for the train.
You kept me just long enough
So that I would have to come back to you again

Out of the dark, as if I was in love
Again, as if I could ever come back in love.

Answering the Emperor Julian
Mesopogon, after Cavafy

His face was ugly in a dozen ways. That's why
As soon as possible he grew the beard
To blur, to soften it. In time the "shrubbery"
Concealed his harelip and his crooked jaw,
And then the wiry throat, the pitted chest,
And combed out like an apron, grey and brown,
In middle age it hid the belly too,
Hid his desire, he combed and combed it.
Yet the face certainly was ugly still: the nose
Sunken, his left eye also. Ugly—but, in a sense,
No matter. He was different, he could not despise
The pauper, the halt, the leper and the man
Whose heart was broken on the horn of love.
(His heart was broken on the horn of love.)
Though he was emperor, he knew what it was like
To be subjected, knew what it could mean
To have your suppliants laughing in their sleeves
And not to be the god of your own temple.
Though they bowed down before him, touched the ground,
The rich, the poor, as his procession passed,
Once out of sight they sneered and blew their lips
Because of his nose and eyes, and more because
He wore that vast ridiculous coarse beard. Also
Because, unlike their previous kings, he knew them.

Triangulation

St John's and Reykjavik, St John's and Shannon:
A blue triangle, see it fill with shoals,
Some whales, the floes of ice, and seven ships,
Sea birds, honeycombs of sunlight, then
Dark in pie segments assembling a vast
Night, and from the north a giant disc of moon
Anarchic, starts to rise
Out of the mountain where hermits kneel
Statue-like, all bowed before
A queen's great absence now become white light.

After Hours

i.

And then, to tell the truth, I didn't much care.
I'd done my time and over. I wanted out.
Just as I was going they summoned me back.
The dumb thing is, I went. They offered money.
I had money enough; yet, when they added
You can keep your office and title, stupid,
I agreed. On short time I sit in the same
Chair at the same table, work piled before me;
Colleagues patronize me, I'm still *Professor*
Without professing, a spiderless cobweb,
While outside the sun climbs through the trees and time's
Not a clock but seasons, the kind an old man
Requires to make peace and walk into the woods
Like a pioneer, released from the routines
Of culture and employment. I didn't think
I cared, and then I stayed and the one who said
I've had enough walked away and wrote me off.

ii.

Good riddance, then. But I can't help wondering
Who he was, what he took with him, where he went.
I sit in the same chair at the work table
And think of him, not enviously. Did he go
To Cornwall where I thought I'd one day settle
In Fowey or Polruan, and walk the cliffs
At the end of England and the end of life
Loving the clouds and even the loud seagulls?
Did he go to Mexico and make a place,
Brief, perhaps, but radiant and very raw,
Having thrown his books and papers on the skip,
An Alp of literature, and chosen mountains,

Real mountains, the pine and cactus, coyotes
And gopher snakes, grey eagles, *zopilotes,*
And *ocote* smoke, pots of red rice, black beans
Hot on the brazier, at night so many stars
He found his place and gave up the glad ghost there . . .
Did he stay at home, his Alp of literature
Intact, wearing his Millet Myo Velcro
Climbing shoes, making his way with hiking poles,
Mammut Galaxy superdry climbing rope,
Crag-climbing gloves, crampons, ice-axes, ice-screws,
Leaving a sequence of huts and bivouacs
As he climbed the texts. Does he reach a summit?
And there in thin air does he find wings and rise?
Is heaven that way? To tell the truth, I care
For him, for all of him, cliff, star and summit.

   iii.

His time is never up. I close my eyes, he's
There for sure, wearing my face, sunburned, windburned,
He's written me off, so he never chides me.
I walk in his prints through the thick cliff edge grass
Or up the flinty *cendero* to the stars,
Or through deep snow and out across the ice fields.
My selves disown me but they remain my selves
Though my feet are dry, my hands clean, and I sit
In precisely the same chair at this table,
Fingering my Mammut Galaxy super
-Dry climbing rope, wondering, will it take my weight?

Death of the Novel

At Preston Station, Yevgeny Bazarov
Gave up the ghost. Having found his Russian heart,
A medical vocation, just starting out
For real, becoming good against his nature,
He died. My train was late again and the snow
Drifted across the platform. Closing the book,
I brushed the ice off of my cheeks, blew my nose.
I stamped my boots to get the circulation
Going, and so returned to the present tense.
Thomas Buddenbrook—at the height of summer,
Arriving at St Pancras, the evening light
In prisms playing on steel, slate and brickwork—
Clamped his rotting teeth. His heart stopped and he slumped
Beside me. I folded him away. I lost
Anna Karenina under the station
Clock in Baltimore. Speeding to Paris, Swann,
I abandoned you. The train had broken down
Just outside Turin when Gerald Crich arrived
At the hollow basin of snow, slipped, and fell,
"And as he fell something broke in his soul, and
Immediately he went to sleep." I have lost
On trains, at stations, so many characters,
Don Quixote, Mrs Ramsay, Nepomuk
A mere child, Little Dombey counting the waves,
Nell, and Mesdames Bovary first and second,
Sweet Madame de Renal and her luminous
Glow worm. And worse, the very worst, Hurstwood, who,
Ragged and spent, in his small cold room, began
"To take off his clothes, but stopped first with his coat,
And tucked it along the crack under the door . . .
After a few moments, in which he reviewed
Nothing, but merely hesitated, he turned
The gas on again, but he applied no match."

On his tombstone Norman Douglas had them carve,
Omnes eodem cogimur, we all reach
The same bourn. His final words, in character:
"Get these fucking nuns away from me."

                             They die
Also, the authors, turning not into ghosts
Like ordinary pilgrims, but into stories
As real, if they wrote truly, as what they wrote.
Stevenson, for instance, still young when he died,
Is told and retold. Henry James adored him,
Man and boy, savouring him in his own words,
Reshaping him as his song, "a child of air
That lingers in the garden there . . ." Samoa
Made him Tusitala, Teller. There he died,
Decanting a good bottle of Burgundy.
Omnes eodem. Conrad called on his friend
Stephen Crane at Dover. It was Crane's last day
In England. He lay in a hotel bedroom
"With a large window looking on to the sea.
He had been very ill and Mrs Crane was
Taking him to some place in Germany.
But one glance at that wasted face was enough
To tell me it was the most forlorn of hopes."
Crane said, "I am tired." Then he said, "Give my love
To your wife and child." Looking back from the door,
"I saw he had turned his head on the pillow."
Conrad watched from the threshold, noting how "he
Was staring out of the window at the sails
Of a cutter yacht that glided slowly like
A dim shadow against the grey sky." He pulled
The sea around him, tight around his shoulders.
It was cold.

              I stamp my boots. The train arrives.

Towards Monte Alban

High on the hill shanties catch
The day's first rays, not hot at all,
That dazzle, the ignition
Of white things, blades of glass, of tin
And clothes hung out (the poor are
The cleanest people, always). Eyes
Open pearl white, the iris
Sapphire. Eyes open pearl white on
The day's one good minute.
                              Sun
Goes downhill after that to a
Descending chorus of cock
Crows, little birds jump from their nests.
The near hills shift to distance.
What is close and is not clean and
Cannot dazzle clarifies.
Light dulls to haze. It's eight o'clock,
The shrill knife grinder rides by.
Heads down, the cocks are plucking dust.

Homage to Dr Atl

Gerardo Murillo (1875-1964), pictor, depicter of Iztaccihuatl and Popocatepetl

Was it really so lurid, so anarchic,
Dr Atl? Your palette persuaded you.
Those macaw-shrill floes, eruptions, impastos:
Apocalypse, then a primeval sunrise;
Geological eviscerations, ooze,
Blooms; among tuffa, obsidian blades: that's what
You saw, and your own eyes deeper, bloodshot, year
By year. Enormous canvases. If only
You could have scaled them up to the horizon!
What did you prop them against or fix them to
As you splattered them with vision?
                                        Made blind by
"That mountain Medusa" with his tangle beard
Who hopped on one leg, crag to crag, I soon fled
(As soon as it was decent) the "Retrospect"
At the Muséo de Arte Moderno.
It was the long night of the 1960s.
I stumbled through the dark and off the pathways
Bathing my eyes clear in the garden fountains
And the sweet shadows of Chapultepec. How
Moderno were you, nineteenth-century, impure
Romantic of a world free of men, amen.

Yet the mountains were bodies you made love to.
Eros of pigment, Gerardo, how you slept
With them, on them, like Donne's am'rous flea fastened
To their skirts, their skin, your tiny bivouacs,
The wandering flare of your nightly campfires,
Corn cakes, tubs of bitter coffee, pots of broth;
Steep canvases dried by the fire's play of heat
And shadow, and you slept, your mouth to the rock,
Your little heart drumming the mountain's giant
Breast, *let me in, let me in,* and it let you
Lie there in the scrub with your lips on its heart.

Can a simple century have so rendered down
To monochrome? Today, certainly, flying
Over your habitat, your landscapes' contours
Drawn steeply up by the sun falling, haze is
All the residual bloom the mountains have,
And slow tumble of fumes from the crater's mouth
Downhill, dilating sulphur into a smog
Of the poisons of a world of men, amen.

The Education of Henry Adams, Private Secretary
Mansfield Street, Portland Place, London
—Towards a Cento

    i.

Once only he saw Mr. Lincoln.
Washington, midnight, at winter's end,
A melancholy Inaugural
Ball, waltzes off-key, spurs, spittoons, and
Him a long plain figure among gowns:
Ploughed face, an air funereal in part
Due to a habit of foreboding,
In part to his too-tight beige kid-gloves.
No man in the Republic required
(He grimaced, saying it of himself)
More instruction than the President.

Lincoln, Seward, Sumner could not help
The greenhorn Private Secretary
With his slow *Education*; why, *they*
Knew as little as he did! (All through
The memoir his "I" is "he.") He'd read
Six long years of Law; they'd practiced it
And what they did would cost ten thousand
Million dollars and a million lives.

On April thirteen Fort Sumter fell,
The storm burst, its lightning and thunder
Rolling several hundred thousand young
Men and Henry Adams in the surf
Of a wild ocean, all helpless as
He was but not all safe. He had time
To go observe the regiments form
Ranks by the Boston State House, gather
In the solemn April evening and

Start the march south, with the docile frowns
They'd practiced to perfection from birth.
No drums and fifes, no kind of fanfare.
He had time to go down afterwards
To the port and embrace his brother
Charles, safe-quartered for the time being
In Fort Independence, the Army
Of the Republic falling into
Line around him, boots, belts and weapons,
In resolute blue rows, their numbers
Called. Nothing was so trivial that night
As the Private Secretary in
The dark, crawling down to the Cunard
Steamboat *Niagara* to sail again
With his father the Minister for
England.

    ii.

      In London Secretary
Adams carried messages, took tea,
Dictation, copied and recopied
Letters, betweentimes inching through Law
Through Blackstone, like a termite through oak.
He suffered waking nightmares. The old
Duchess Dowager of Somerset,
A harridan with castanets, forced
The Turkish Ambassador's daughter
To perform a Highland fling with him.
The gentry smirked, clapped, and stamped their feet.
That night his pride came home in ashes.

He took for granted that his business
Was obedience, discipline, silence.
He never labored so hard to learn
A language as he did to hold his

Tongue, and it affected him for life.
A habit of reticence—talking
Without meaning—cannot be broken.

In his loneliness, when the story
Of Bull Run appeared in *The Times*, he
Hugged himself tight, felt a pang so deep,
Of his own absence from the one real
Story, that he was sick for a week.
He kept the door bolted. To be dead
With—no one knew the final number.
To be dead! And, breathing, he was dead.
Bull Run. The cause was lost. The English
Predicted history the moment
They recognized the South. Quite soon
They'd draw the line, do the final sums.
Events happened over there, the charge,
Retreat, flags in the mud, the bodies
Heaped, the carts and mules. But history
Happens at a distance, happens here
Where blood dries to ink. Minutiae,
Passions, amputations, don't survive
The transit from pain to history.
The subject burns down with the houses,
The soft goods, clocks and shifts, the bird cage.
Chimneys survive, memorializing—
One, two, three, four, five—the avenue.

What might have happened if he hadn't
Taken his father's counsel and flown
The coop, a Private Secretary?
Instead like men in uniform, in
Flames, alive or dead, and not a scribe
Reading the consequences of what
Should have been his story inscribed by
Thucydides.

iii.

               Two years on, July,
In Pennsylvania. The bell's not chimed.
The rail fence holds, summer fields, the woods
Stand hospitable. The patient blue
And gray brigades find the countryside
Foreign as Palestine or Britain.
They stand to, tense, flags tight-furled, breeze still.
It has not happened yet. If I don't
Put pen to paper, need it happen?
The Private Secretary dries the
Nib. Primed, on the mantle shelf the clock
Whirs, the English air waits for eight chimes.
(The voice of Longstreet rises in his
Throat, Kemper is sallow, grave Wilcox
Feels his heart dive like a fish. A jet
Of shrill sunlight bursts from Pickett's sword.)

The Private Secretary survives
A dream of bayonets. He lies stiff.
Time to go home, father, time to go.
Which his father answers with a stare
Open and empty.
                  Whitman wrote how
In some cemeteries north and south
Nearly *all* the dead are Unknown. At
Salisbury, North Carolina, the
Known are only eighty-five, the un-
Known twelve thousand and twenty-seven.
Eleven thousand seven hundred
Of these are buried in the furrows
The war ploughed in Lincoln's patient brow.

iv.

Many a shock was Henry Adams
To meet in the course of a long life
Spent with politicians, politics.
The profoundest lessons are not those
Of reason: they're sudden strains that warp
The mind for good. It's a dismal school
Because the lessons never finish,
The war continues as the plough turns
Up in the fields new skulls, evidence
That numbers change. No name gets added.

Sherman's Georgia

i.

No one will tell the story straight.
What's there to tell it with but words?
They, too, are ruined, like the row
Of chimneys, hearths and fireplaces
Poking out of a mess of thorns
And evergreen. By the jetty
Where the trees are lame, they lean to
One another. Moss beards extend,
Floating on green water. Weeds and
Water weeds stink, high on summer.

ii.

I lean an elbow on a mantle shelf
Warmed by sun. In the old days it was fire.
Looking through a room my great-grandfather
Looked into, and knocked his pipe, and squatted
To prod the coals, I see a space furnished
With hairy rattleweed full of spiders,
Coneflowers, quillwort, dropwort, several
Sumacs, stunted rue and campion, pungent
Nutmeg, confederate wake-robin, a
Feathering silk tree, love in a puff, nut-
Sedge and lilac bell, cocklebur that killed
The livestock off, the purple, velvet or
The sandy sedge.
                    July the first. I was
Sixteen in 1963. It was
Striking two o'clock. I found evidence:
Still a house of sorts, my great-grandfather's
Property, tumbled walls, the shapes of rooms,
Doorsteps, stone outlasted the wood, withstood

The flames that took the avenue. The wood
And cotton burned, and all the rest of it.
No one tells the story. 2012.
The land's been cleared, the step swept clean away.

The Stories of My Life

i. Marginalia

By candle-light, the wavering text.
The pen he drives above the words
A wing in flight, its urgent pulse
In dialogue with what he reads
(As ventricle with ventricle
Exchanges confidence and blood,
Telltale and intimate, profane),
Its nib a beak, its nib a noise
Of rookeries, of pinions.
Out of the crystal pool it drinks,
Its voice is black . . . his lips make shapes
Of sound, his tongue tip like a kiss.

He frowns and notes, "In getting books
I always seek a margin wide
As possible," and this is for
"Comments, agreements, differences."
If there's too little space he puts
"A slip of paper between leaves
Secured by imperceptible
Portions of gum tragacanth paste."

He talks in whispers to himself,
"Freshly, boldly, without conceit."
That's how his "cynosures" communed
With God and Nature in old times,
Taylor, Temple, Thomas Browne,
"The anatomical Burton,
And Butler, that most logical
Analogist." Their styles possessed
"A richly marginalic air."

From these alert, immediate flights
His essays grow, his tales arise
Like Pandemonium from the dark
Exhaled, and Lucifer close by.
Into a text he plummets, soars,
And moonless rides its hurling waves;
Returning, perches on a plinth
And croaks his chilling negatives.

"Cover your nose," says Henry James.
Poe is provincial, sulphurous,
Employing "vitriol for ink,"
"And yet . . ." So the concessions start.

Reading the tidy notes and runs
Precisely penned, as if a scribe
From Gower's stone scriptorium
Had travelled centuries to scratch
The tiny clarities, and sow
The seeds of stories, essays, poems,
The sense comes of a man enslaved
By that "new nation" (not so new):
What might it say if moral terms
Took a fresh turn? The frayed homespun,
The bold primeval, street satire,
And patriotic garbage too
Were effortful and treacherous.
What might inherence give rise to?

In his cold flickering studio
Visit his windows on the night,
Frames with their inked out canvases
Emitting melodies, not sense;
Pain, pleasure no analysis
Can circumscribe or make disclose
In paraphrase a prose idea.
He stayed poor. His wife was dying.

He stayed poor and she died, a girl
He loved. His poems envisaged death.
It came, it went. No Orpheus,
And nothing said and nothing meant
And nothing say and nothing mean
Except the spell you cast and what
A spell can conjure out of naught.

ii. *"I love all men who dive."*

"At nightfall Nantucket natives, out of sight
Of land, furl their sails, and lay them to their rest,
While under their very pillows rush the herds
Of walruses and whales." That's where he started.

In 1849 he wrote to Duyckinck:
"I have been passing my time pleasurably,
Chiefly in lounging on a sofa (à la
The poet Grey) & reading Shakespeare, the book
In glorious great type, every letter whereof
Is a soldier, & the top of every 'T'
Like a musket barrel." At day school, textbooks
Had been the squinting, crammed and cheap editions
Printed to make verse mind-numbing for "scholars,"
Preparing them for the calculable worlds
Of lumber, harvest, bullion, prayer, timepieces,
Addition, and addition, profit, power.
Poetry, needlework, pianoforte
Were things girls did, refinements, added polish.
When it came to books, he was like other boys.
"My eyes were tender as young sparrows." But now
On the gangway of the *Pequod*, as it were,
He "chanced to fall in with this edition, I
Exult in it, page after page."
                              Two years on,
To Duyckinck too, he told a happy story.

"I rise at eight—thereabouts—go to my barn—
Say good-morning to the horse, & give him his
Breakfast, pay a visit to my cow. —After,
I go to my work-room & light my fire—then
Spread my manuscript on the table—take one
Business squint at it, & fall to with a will."
Five hours on the high seas, and then a knock,
He feeds the animals, dines, then rigs the sleigh,
Starts for the village, with mother or sisters.
"Evenings, in my room, unable to read, I
Spend in a mesmeric state, skimming over
Some large-printed book." There was Shakespeare again,
His Virgil, pouring him through Hell's dark funnel.

More years: the inkwell dry, the page dry, his eyes
Sting. *Pequod*, Queequeg and his faith are all drowned.
The sharks, so fierce before, are now unharming,
"With padlocks on their mouths"; the silent sea-hawks
"Sail with sheathed beaks." And last, the good ship *Rachel*
Misses her bobbing child and sets with the moon.

Not to Duyckinck now, with just his lips moving
He tells himself, "You have not spared Ishmael.
You know what you have done and know how it's true,
You know the Saviour perished, but not for him."
Thumbing the manuscript. "This. Your book of ends.
You are exhausted with thrashing up and down
The watery paragraphs, now your hour's come.
But things don't finish as they ought, that's the way
The Fall refashioned the world, we each hang from
A cross we make for ourself; we drive the spikes
With an oak mallet into our palms and wrists,
Into our shins, right there above the heel-bone,
On some companionless Calvary, some whale-
Humped hill without the thieves or the three Maries,
Only the spear, sharp as a humming-bird's beak

Finding the heart's rose; and, rising to the lips
Like a kiss, a kiss, the sponge of vinegar."

So he could tell the story at all, he must
Distort the truth, turn the good ship *Rachel* back
To hear the call (a necessary conceit,
As though the voice of a chosen child survived
The waves of flame in Ahab's pitch Gehenna),
"I'm Ishmael, survivor of the *Pequod*.
I am Jonah, survivor of the white whale."

   iii. Hearsay

And Whitman? You never read his *Leaves*?
"But they told me he was disgraceful."
Disgraceful? Now consider yourself!
Your life first offered on convention's
Happy altar, then snatched meanly back.
Your book too, like his, is appalling,
Miasmic, it changes with each reading,
Etching the living bone with diamond.

Your life was uneventful only
In the sense that no events attach
The vivid crises of your poems.
You lived out the War Between the States:
Rumors, the declaration, tolling,
Men mustered, parading in your street,
The tearful ritual of departure . . .
You stood, shadow, in the open door.
Then the wounded came home, and the dead
In boxes, as ghosts, or not at all.
Missing, you waited for the missing,
For twenty years, patiently, after
The war was done, in your snowy dress,

In your anxious room, as a widow
Knows what cannot be and yet it is:
Feel his breath, a light kiss on the nape.

Or you wait for Christ. Never a first
Communion, it's unction you wait for.
If only your knees would bend! Autumn
Buried by solving snow. No spring.
Saint Teresa knew what you learned, too:
In the particulars of this world
Only, if at all, can His wounds, His
Love be inferred, the transcendent *Hoc*
Est, or not at all. Inherences,
Or untenanted from *fiat lux*
For ever. The heart flutters, rises,
White as a petal bride, along aisles
Of moonlight . . . where's the groom? . . . she's seeking
His bloody cross beam to alight on,
But finds no thief bad or good, no Christ.

iv. "the dark corners, the closed rooms"

He learned to be a Puritan in winter.
The plain parlor of the house where he grew up
In Salem, Massachusetts—outside, deep snow,
Within, a family by candle-light, and
Open on the table the prints of Flaxman,
Black on white, figures from Homer and Dante,
Sharp, suggestive templates which every viewer
Invests with hue and texture, tell their story.
The widow turns the pages and the children
Crane, question; they share the chaste stuttering light.
At the same time the boy takes something private,
Sensual to heart, so that when the fire's raked
Safe in the hearth, the candles snuffed and the house
Asleep, in his chamber, with the door bolted,

In the tumbled bed he lolls with her, and her,
Andromache or Dido, the Pleiades
Gracious, approaching, smelling of snow and stars.
He releases each heroine from her story,
Removes her robes and, clothing her with desire,
Banks night after night the furtive ecstasies
And the incremental guilt that Hester Prynne
Is the most artless and aberrant child of.
His darker thoughts are luminous. Like a cat
He sees in the dark. Like a demon he watches
Darkness herself shake out her abundant hair.

"If ever I should have a biographer,
He ought to make great mention of this chamber.
So much of my lonely youth was wasted here,
Waiting patiently for the world to know me . . ."
It came to know him, he married happily.
He turned his haunting ancestors to fiction.
To his friend Bridge in 1850 he joked
How he'd finished his book "yesterday; one end
Being in the press at Boston, the other
In my head here at Salem, so my story
Is at least fourteen miles long . . ."
                              American,
Abroad for years, he could not really explain
What it meant, or why he was "always outside
Everything," as Henry James said, an "alien
Everywhere, an aesthetic solitary."
The Marble Faun marked his last transformation,
But as before, he did not quite understand
What it meant to disclose, it might have been love.

Back at that Salem window, looking in now,
A December bird, he observes the widow,
Album, siblings—but the boy has disappeared.
Banished, or set free? Reluctantly he clings,
As if caught in bird lime, to the sill. "There seem

Things I can almost get hold of, think about;
But when I am on the point of seizing them,
They start away, like slippery things." He is snared
And plucked and seasoned. His language gropes, things and
Nothings. Too late he's come back home, all's altered.

I know the house of course . . .

But who're the seven Gables? *First, papá,*
His portrait in the hall, his portrait in
The library, on the fat chimney breast
In the drawing room, in the pantry too,
Thumbs in his waistcoat, thumbs hooked in his coat,
Thumbs in his trouser pockets; here at last,
The tower bedroom, framed in ebony,
Flabbergasted, fingers in his ears.

First papá, the trail of portraits climbs. He
Down in the garden meanwhile, worsted rump
Busy among vegetables interspersed
With acanthus, rose, with peonies, sweet
Peas, convolvulus, all bleached by summer.
This year's Carrara columns: polished leeks;
This year, Carrara, the white potatoes,
The pale, smudged turnips, bleached asparagus.

In no portrait are his hands as dirty
As they are here, a fist of marl, grim loam,
Manure, gravel, compost, the torn tendrils
Of what the books call weeds (they call them weeds!);
His thumbs, thick as hummingbirds, are busy
About some business, dig, eviscerate,
Impale. Beside him in Paradise three
Robins triangulate, suing for worms.

Who are the seven Gables? *Meet papá.*
We've met papá. But where's Mrs Gable?
His son? His three fat daughters? Uncle Drew?
You've met papa, the house's metonym.

The Stove

. . . and kisses on the rowan tree
the scarlet ulcers of the unseen Christ.
—Sergei Esenin, 'Autumn'
(translated by Geoffrey Thurley)

In the big round stove they're burning up the trees.
It's hot all day in the tall kitchen. Outside
It's freezing, it's sunless as if a shadow was cast
By the ghosts of the trees that are burning, and the stove
Stays glowing all day, even when nobody's by.
They're burning the trees. All over mother Russia
The forests burn. Her face is grimed with soot.

They're not big trees but thin sticks of birch they're burning,
The graceful wings of pine and spruce, the blood-berried rowan.

Poem
23 March 2003

      i.

Mountains, rivers, waves of grain, red deserts, oceans!
Fifty stars, and not a single sun.

      ii.

Who writes the history? There is no war,
No victory or victor.
                        Separation, hearsay,
Gossip, innuendo, rumor
Whispered until there is a conjuration,
A demon spins into view and now
There has to be a war, and she the victim
Holds behind her back a scimitar,
Froth of blood still on it, and intones
How it has been, lays out the fresh wounds
Side by side like fish on a market slab.

ARCHEOLOGY

Anacreon
After the Greek

i.

Again I love again I do not love
Am mad again and am not mad again.

ii.

I'm grey on the sides and white on top;
Youth that was nimble is gone, my teeth themselves
Ache and chatter, life's span is shortening, and I
Sigh more than sometimes, fearing Tartarus;
The dark forks of Hell hold terrors for me
And the pathway drops precipitate and once
A man starts down there's no way back.

iii.

Observe him, old Anacreon, frayed and worn, wobbly
With wine, how he bends his shape into the stone.
     He gazes, look at him, with eyes that look
     With love, with lust, and see too how his gown
Trails right down to his heel. In a haze of wine
He's lost one sandal, but the other still conceals
     A shriveled clutch of toes. The poet sings
     Of charming Bathyllus, full-fleshed Megistus
And he's strumming his melancholy lyre. O Muses,
Keep him safe, for it would be wrong indeed
     Were Bacchus' faithful servant to be felled
     By Bacchus' wine.

The Husband's Message
From the Old English

To you far away   I carry this message
I remain true   to the tree I was hacked from
Wood I am, bearing   the marks of a man
Letters and runes   the words of his heart
I come from afar   borne on salt currents
Hiss . . .   in a hull I sought and I sought you
Where would I find you   my lord dispatched me
Over fathomless seas   I've come, here I am
Do you think of him still   my lord in your dear heart
Do you recall him   or is your mind bare
He remains true to you   true and with fixed desire
You try his faith   you'll find it stands firm

But hear me now, read   what is scratched on my surface

You, cherished treasure, dear   you in your youthful
Your hidden heart, dear   remember your vows
Your heart and his heart   when together you haunted
The lovely hamlets   the mead hall, the promise
To perform your love.
                    Well, all of that ended
In feud and in flight   he was forced from that place.
Now he has sent me   to ask you *come to me*
Cross the seas, come to me   come here with joy
When to your listening   on the steep hillside
First comes the cuckoo's voice   sad in the trees
Don't pause don't linger   come at that calling
Don't stay or delay   come at that call
Go down to the shore   set out to sea then
To the tern's chilly home   go south go south
Over the ragged sea   south find your lord
Come to him, there   he waits for you wedded
To your sure arrival   no other wish

But only the wish of you   You're more in his mind
Than Almighty God   whose power could bind you
One to the other   again as you were
Able to rule then   able to raise up
Your people, comrades   and endow you with jewels
Bracelets and carcanets   collars and combs
He has set aside for you   fair gold, bright gemstones
In a faraway land   among foreign folk
A handsome mansion   hectares and cattle
Faithful retainers
                        though when he set out
Pursued and a pauper   he pointed his prow
Out to the sea   alone set out sailing
Lost in his exile   yet eager to go
Weaving the currents   time in his veins

Now truly that man   has passed beyond pain
He has all he wants   has horses, has treasure
The great hall's warm welcome   gifts the earth yields
Princess, Princess   you too are his portion
Remember the promises   each of you vowed
The sealing silences   he made and you made
A letter, a syllable   nothing is lost
What seem erasures   are kisses and praying
Are runes that keep counsel   a promise in touch
A promise in looking   how staunch he has stayed to you
Above him the heavens   the earth under foot
A man of his word he is   true to your contract
The twining of wills   in those days gone in time

In this Modest Style
from the Spanish of Ramón López Velarde

It's how she spreads, without a sound, perfume
of orange blossom on the dark of me,
it's the way she shrouds in mourning black
her mother of pearl and ivory, the way
she wears the lace ruff at her throat, and how
she turns her face, quite voiceless, self-possessed,
because she takes the language straight to heart,
is thrifty with the words she speaks.

It's how

She's so reticent yet welcoming
when she comes out to face my panegyrics,
the way she says my name
mocking and mimicking, makes fun,
but she knows that my unspoken drama
is really of the heart, though a little silly;
it's how, when night is deep and at its darkest,
we linger after dinner, indistinctly talking
and her laughing smile grows fainter and then drops
softly on the table cloth; it's her teasing, the way
she won't give me her arm and then allows
passion to chaperone us when we walk out,
when we promenade on the hot colonial boulevard . . .

Because of this, your whispered, modest style
of love, I worship you, my faithful star.
You like to cloud yourself in mourning,
And give, my hidden blossom; kindly,
Mellow, you have presided over
my thirty years with the self-effacing concentration
of a vase whose half-blown roses wreathe in scent
the headboard of a convalescent man;
cautious nurse, shy
serving maid, dear friend who trembles

with the trembling of a child when you revise
the reading that we share; apprehensive, always timid
guest at the feast I give; my apprehensive ally,
humble dove that coos when it is morning
in a minor key, a key that's wholly yours.

I beatify you, modest, magnificent;
you have possessed the highest summit of my heart,
you who are at once the artist
of lowly and most lofty things, who bear in your hands
my life as if it was your work of art!

O star and orange blossom, may you go
lightly swayed in an unwedded peace,
and may you dwindle like a morning star
which the lightening greenness of a meadow darkens
or like a flower that finds transfiguration
on the blue west, as it might on a single bed.

September 1915

Quartet (Quarteto)

From the Spanish of Octavio Paz

> *Ore, fermate il volo*
> *nel lucido oriente,*
> *mentre s'en vola il ciel rapidamente*
> *e, carolando intorno*
> *a l'alba mattutina*
> *ch'esce da la marina,*
> *l'umana vita ritardate e'l giorno.*
> *—Tasso*

i.

Known yet always strange, the lie of the land,
the riddle of the palm of one's own hand.
The ocean sculpts in each wave, stubbornly,
the monument in which it falls away.
Against the sea, a will that's turned to rock,
the faceless headland keeps the sea in check.
The clouds: they are inventing sudden bays
where a plane is a skiff that melts away.
The rapid scribbling of the birds above
others are fishing where the waters move.
Between the sea-foam and the sand I tread,
the sun is resting light upon my head:
between what's static and what will not stay
in me the elements enact their play.

ii.

There are tourists also on this strand,
death in a bikini, death with jewelled hand,
there are rumps and bellies, loins, lungs, thighs,
a cornucopia of bland enormities,
a scattered abundance that precedes
the meal of ashes where the worm will feed.
Adjacent, yet divided by those lines
strictly kept but tacit, undefined,
are vendors, and the stalls where fries are sold,
and panders, parasites, untouchables,
the rags of poor men and the poor man's bones.
The rich are stingy while the poor man fawns:
God loves them not, nor do they love themselves:
"each does but hate his neighbour as himself."[1]

iii.

The wind breaks forth and gathers up the grove,
the nations of cloud disperse above.
The real is fragile, wavering, unsure
also, its law is change, it does not tire.
Round and round the wheel of seemings spins
upon a fixity: the axis time.
Light sketches all and then turns all to flame,
with daggers that are brands it stabs the main
and makes the world a pyre of mirrorings:
we are mere white horses of the sea.
It's not Plotinus's light, it's earthly light,
a light of here, but it is thoughtful light.
It brings, between me and my exile, peace:
my home this light, its shifting emptiness.

---

1 Alexander Pope

iv.

To wait for nightfall, I have stretched myself
under the shadow of a throbbing tree.
The tree is a woman in whose leaves
I hear the ocean roll beneath noon heat.
I eat her fruits that have the taste of time,
fruits of forgetfulness, fruits of wisdom.
Beneath the tree, the images and thoughts
and words regard each other, touch.
Through the body we return where we began,
spiral of stillness and of motion.
To taste, to know—it is finite, this pause:
it has beginning, end—is measureless.
Night enters and it rolls us in its wake;
the sea repeats its syllables, now black.

Anacreontea
After the Greek

i.

Beloved swallow, every year you come,
You weave a nest in Summer, then you're off,
Wintering near the Nile, at Memphis.
In my heart Eros, not regarding seasons,
Keeps weaving a nest, where one
Longing is fledgling, another still in egg,
A third just hatching; and the nest is loud
With wide-beaked chicks all clamoring for food.
The larger feed the baby Longings,
And when they are mature there in my heart
They themselves, in Eros' nest, begin begetting.
What am I to do, I am too old, too weak
To shout to silence this vast flock of Longings.

ii.

Anacreon, the Teian singer, in a dream
Saw and called to me. I ran and kissed him.
I hugged him. He was old but still quite handsome
And Love was working in him, the wine scented
His lips. Since he was old, unstable on his pins,
Eros clutched his hand and guided him.
The poet lifted from his brows the garland
And passed it to me, and it smelled of him.
I was a foolish boy, I placed it
On my own head as a crown, and ever since
I've not lived a single moment without love.

DIVINE POEMS

Anniversary

When I am sleeping things occur. You come
Back from the dead, I lift the big stone off you
With my dream fingers, it weighs no more than a feather.
You stand and stretch and look, though not at me
Because I am asleep. You walk right through me.
You leave prints in the dirt and your shadow
Moves close beside you, shadow cast by moonlight,
As though an intimate has come back with you
Holding your hand, sharing your pulse and posture.
You have upon you the smell of mildew and soil
And that sweetness you always wore is palpable and yes,
You walk right through me and I feel your heart again
Pommelling the bone bars inside your chest
And in your throat and lungs the rasping that killed you
Not the phlegmy prelude to your funeral,
More now like a hoarse hymn of resurrection.
Down at the cemetery gate you linger,
Step out into the road with its yellow lamps,
Look, your shadow also, towards town, then up hill.
No one familiar. No one, not even a car.
You turn and come back in, and go back home
To the place we put you, marked, and in time forgot,
Walking right through me you find the spot
Among the pine shrubs, by the wind-shaped oak,
Lie down again and pull the soil tight up
Under your chin, and close your hazel eyes.
The big stone weighs too much for me, your shadow
Helps me replace it and daylight comes in.

Also, Poor Yorick

Yorick's heart is moved: how beautiful, he says,
And grasps then what it must mean to be human
Returning rested from the afterlife
Into the lovely dew of resurrection.
Bare feet, with the worms and roots still in them,
The puddles cool between their metatarsals.

The skulls bay with joy, and all are grinning,
Popping their knuckles, counting their vertebrae,
And now they dance alone and now join hands,
And as they dance there, in their ribs and rigging
In each grey skeleton a robin perches
Plumping its feathers, pulsing out its song

Red, and the twittering's blood as well as music.
—Never has he witnessed a scene so vital,
The dance of life the scripture guaranteed.
Faster as shadows shorten and noon rises
The skeletons spin and conga into the air
Making a cloud, a halo on the sun.

He takes his spade and sets it on his shoulder.
He's old. Till now he's known so much regret.
He's buried his grandparents and his parents,
His kings and queens, his brothers and his friends,
His lovers, all of them, consumables,
Pulvis, cinis, nihil, the bones bearing

In their chalk wholeness so much love and light.
In his own graveyard, with the dear departed
One unfamiliar skeleton stands up
Tall, gracious, folding down his finger bones
Over two holes; where his hurt feet strike stone,
Sparks from the rusty nails, and in his side

A spear, perch for a phoenix. Jesus Christ
Risen in this garden, and the wounds,
Or the bones that keep the marks of wounds, are singing.
It's noon, there are no shadows. This is true.
He raised them and himself is rising up.
Also, poor Yorick. That was judgement, it is over.

Later in the day the Prince arrives,
Stepping from his script as from a carriage
Drawn up among the holes in which the dead
Waited, and from which they are all delivered,
Just like an audience when the play is over
Elbowing their coats into the dark.

Anxious, a bit deranged, he finds occasion
To hold a conversation with a skull.
Is it a skull or a stone that looks like a skull?
The heads are all gone to heaven, Jesus too,
The sexton himself put off his flesh and followed.
(Ophelia was already on her star.)

Poor prince, alone with just a book of ballads,
With just the plot nothing can raise him from.

Guo Nian
Shānyáng? Miányáng?

Is it the year of the sheep, the goat, the antelope?
I'm confused, and you who should know because
It is your calendar, and language is your subject,
Say with a smile, *It's a problem of translation,*
And that's the end of it! But I want to know
Is it the year of the billy, buck, hogget or ram,
The nanny, the wether, the kid, the silver chevron?
Of blubbery mutton? Or is it the year of the lamb?

It is the year of the lamb, the first soft creature
Man brought home and tended and gathered for grazing
On a hill, down shadowy valleys, to the plain,
Reared for its wool, for its music, for its sweet beard,
Herded and led to the fold, kept from the wolf
And tended and slept among at Choga Mami
In Diyarbakir, in Jericho and here in Doggerland.

It's the year of the lamb, the first soft creature
We took to our hearths and hearts and tended, we cared for,
The first creature we reared for coarse cloth and cheeses,
For trust, the merry bleating in upland pastures
And in April, bruised salvia, sage, dew-drenched, at sunrise
We dress it, cense the altar, whetting a paschal razor,
Blood on our wrists, in our gullets, the steaming oblation
That blesses us still as we slit its quavering throat.

Cosimo de' Medici's Commission

Il Beato pinxit.
The deferential angel
Won't leave her alone.
He comes from God and finds her
In a bright loggia
Wistful, beautiful. He lands
Armed with his lily,
A wand her presence magics
Out of sight, a scent,
A spell her shy averted
Pallor, when she looks his way,
Translates into prayer.

This gorgeous angel's
Seen a thing or two: stood guard
In Paradise, watched
The Serpent make sport of Eve,
Published Adam's Fall;
Jerusalem he levelled,
Towers, citizens,
Sweeping Israel's dust into
The ugly mountain
We call Golgotha. He hears
Dull mallets drive the nails in.
He tastes vinegar.

Hail, he murmurs, *grace* . . .
He who's God's sword, God's eagle,
Earlier he's obeyed
Orders, soaring home on gold
Untarnished pinions,
This time something's gone awry.
She bends away, he
Wants her to attend, to touch.

What is this, he says,
Can I become man? No, just
An angel, heavy haloed,
Gold winged, unable.

Wretched Gabriel,
Who tend the orchard of souls,
Plucking from night trees
The spirits we grow into,
Who make prophets hear
Heaven's thunder in their hearts,
Who give Zachary
The stupendous news of Christ,
See her, attentive
To the message your lips say,
But to your gaze? Your honed wings—
Dazzled by desire?

Consider how she
Is just a girl, a pauper.
And how old, angel,
You are: can you count up your
Eternity? She
Could smell, if she desired to,
How your gilded hair,
Handsome cheek, linen singlet,
Mulberry folds, hide
What would be ash if ever
You'd broken bread. You are not
What she'd ever want.

The Wafer
"The Face of Christ," late fifteenth century, Dutch

Each takes a little, east and south and west,
Diminishes it, like nibbling the edge
Of a sweet biscuit, each takes a kiss of crust,
A lip of sugar, a lick of crumbs
Each takes until remaining the blank core
Is mere erasure where His face has been.

On the Morning of Christ's Crucifixion

. . . From haunted spring and dale?
Edg'd with poplar pale,
The parting Genius is with sighing sent,
With flowre-inwov'n tresses torn?
The Nimphs in twilight shade of tangled thickets mourn.
              —From Milton's "On the Morning of Christ's Nativity"

It wasn't at his birth the gods came down.
They didn't know the baby had arrived,
What he'd been, who he was, who he would be.
Olympus was home. For one more generation
They could meddle in the lives of us below,
Cross our true loves, plough our cities under
With war, raise storms, rattle the earth, and after
Return to the lowering clouds and sleep it off,
Starting again next day, as myth prescribed,
And so serve out eternities of mischief.

Not all was mischief there. Mild Vesta swept
Ash from a cloudy hearth, and Janus
Sat on the stoop and watched another morning
Climb the escarpments, molten, and the stars
Dim, then drown like sparks in the rising light.
The Larès were already at work in the barley fields,
Pomona from the orchard brought a skirtful of blossom
And Palès looked after goats in the upper pasture.
Ops and Consus slept in the haystack till harvest.
This is how it was, how it should have been.

Across a sea and in another language
A Roman and a Jew in quiet conversation
Under the wings of a cedar begin to change the world
Rock by fracturing rock, grass blade by blade.
They reach accommodation: Barabbas

Vanishes in the crowd, another captive
Is robed and crowned. He's king. He takes his cross
As men are made to dig out their own graves.
He falls and rises, is scourged, is cursed, is pitied,
He climbs to the summit assigned and is crucified.

Every mountain he has climbed, climbing that mountain.
Every mountain shaken. Rocks tumble down the sides.
Olympus too, where the gods have always lived,
Is beaten like a drum, the light explodes
And even here, as at Jerusalem
A crossbow with a man drawn taut upon it,
Drawn like an arrow aimed straight at the mid-day sun—
And suddenly the sun falls out of the sky.
It's as dark as just before the world was made,
As it will be when time at last is over.

The lights go up again. The crossbow on the summit
Is Christ drawn taut by his own gravity.
An altered sun burns over the whole earth.
Olympus feels it. The old gods are over.
The clouds have let them down. They blame a book
They never read before. They've been at sea: with a clang
Noah drops the enormous gangplank. The ark's grounded
Not on Ararat or Olympus. Golgotha.
Light is transfigured. The gods gather up their belongings.
They start down the broken path in dazzled pairs;

All stiff and molting, mangy with confinement,
Beasts out of the ark after months at sea,
Cawing, croaking, buzzing, growling they stumble.
They have forgotten where on earth they belong,
Seeing it afresh and frowning hard at it.
Now they are subject to the laws of kind.
The yellow rheumy-eyed lion with his glum
Mate is Jupiter. Where's their savanna?
Apollo, no longer brilliant, a wheeling eagle.
Diana bends at a pool and licks the light.

A dove who was Venus coos for her blank-eyed son,
Wherever he flew he's gone. There's lumbering Vulcan
Rutting, the boar he always was; and Mars, she says,
Where is Mars, will we ever again together
Swing in a single snare and be in love?
Mercury, already nesting, is a swallow,
Minerva, a blinking bay-owl, waits for nightfall.
Bacchus and Maia, he stumbling, she supporting,
Begin to bleat and whirr: goat, hummingbird.
After the privilege of Olympus, they are fallen.

> *Not all is altered there. Mild Vesta sweeps*
> *Ashes from the cloudy hearth, and Janus*
> *Sits on the stoop, watches another morning*
> *Climb the escarpments, molten, and the stars*
> *Dim, then drown like sparks in the rising light.*
> *The Larès work in the barley fields, Pomona*
> *Out of the orchard bears a skirtful of blossom.*
> *Palès tends his goats in the upper pasture.*
> *Ops and Consus wake. Is it harvest time?*
> *This is how it is, how it should be.*

Family Tree

Watching his creatures with a filial sorrow
Christ, not a shepherd yet, not yet a man,
Propped on a cloud at the edge of things, his hands,
Unbroken, on his hips, wonders who he'll be
And knows it's up to Adam to determine
What human pleasure might feel like, and what pain,
To the son of God—Adam who's in mourning,
Adam whose Maker has withdrawn the Kingdom
All for a fruit, a serpent and a rib.
The Son of God sees Eve grow plump as a pillow
Bearing a mallet and three nails inside her,
Bearing a spear, a sponge and vinegar.

A Carol for Edward Taylor

after Taylor's meditation on Canticle 1.3. "Thy name is an Ointment poured out"
November 1682: "I have enough. Enough in having thee."

Long fields of yellow wheat
In Palestinian sun
Are ripening into flesh.
The vineyards on the hill
Bring forth a salty fruit.

There where the bread was torn
Off of the human loaf,
Where years began to count
Because a child was born
I come to eat my Word.

Before me at the rail
Is Stephen with the stones
Turned into loaves by love
And James of Zebedee
Carries his singing head;

Peter and Philip bear
Splinters of their cross trees,
Bartholomew his skin
Rolled up beneath his arm,
Thomas from India

With his appalling spear,
And sweet Sebastian too,
God's willing porcupine,
And Agatha whose heart
Is caroling with hurt,

Perpetua with her own new
Baby clutched at her breast,
Felicity her slave
Whose child will not be born
Attended by the beasts

That tore them limb from limb
And slouch now tame and meek
To Bethlehem, and kneel
The way the sheep and ox
Knelt on that first day.

Cyprian and Polycarp
Both try to sneak away
But drawn by the infant Host
Out-dazzling from his crib
The flare of martyrs' fires

(Antipas on the grill—
Domitian's brazen bull,
And all the melting saints
That lit his jubilees,
And later La Pucelle,

And in a northern town
Cranmer and Ridley too,
Transcendent kindling,
Making the tongues of flame
Speak so we understood)

They climb their Calvary
Carrying such precious gifts
As Africa can spare.
There where the wine was spilled
Out of the Virgin's womb

Belief and disbelief,
Faithful and faithless, kneel
Because, whatever's true,
A child is going to grow
On whom we can impress

Fear, hatred and desire,
A child we will impale
And plant in every grave.
We do it by the Book.
I come to eat my Word.

Pangur Bàn

Jerome has his enormous dozy lion.
Myself, I have a cat, my Pangur Bàn.

What did Jerome feed up his lion with?
Always he's fat and fleecy, always sleeping

As if after a meal. Perhaps a Christian?
Perhaps a lamb, or a fish, or a loaf of bread.

His lion's always smiling, chin on paw,
What looks like purring rippling his face

And there on Jerome's escritoire by the quill and ink pot
The long black thorn he drew from the lion's paw.

Look, Pangur, at the picture of the lion—
Not a mouser like you, not lean, not ever

Chasing a quill as it flutters over parchment
Leaving its trail that is the word of God.

Pangur, you are so trim beside the lion.
—Unlike Jerome in the mouth of his desert cave

Wrapped in a wardrobe of robes despite the heat,
I in this Irish winter, Pangur Bàn,

Am cold, without so much as your pillow case
Of fur, white, with ginger tips on ears and tail.

ii.

My name is neither here nor there, I am employed
By Colum Cille who will be a saint

Because of me and how I have set down
The word of God. He pays. He goes to heaven.

I stay on earth, in this cell with the high empty window,
The long light in summer, the winter stars.

I work with my quill and colours, bent and blinder
Each season, colder, but the pages fill.

Just when I started work the cat arrived
Sleek and sharp at my elbow, out of nowhere;

I dipped my pen. He settled in with me.
He listened and replied. He kept my counsel.

iii.

Here in the margin, Pangur, I inscribe you.
Almost Amen. Prowl out of now and go down

Into time's garden, wary with your tip-toe hearing.
You'll live well enough on mice and shrews till you find

The next scriptorium, a bowl of milk. Some scribe
Will recognise you, Pangur Bàn, and feed you;

You'll find your way to him as you did to me
From nowhere (but you sniffed out your Jerome).

Stay by him, too, until his Gospel's done.
(I linger over John, the closing verses,

You're restless, won't be touched. I'm old. The solstice.)
Amen, dear Pangur Bàn. Amen. Be sly.

Jacob and the Angel

And when he saw that he prevailed not against him,
he touched the hollow of his thigh; and the hollow of
Jacob's thigh was strained, as he wrestled with him.
                                   Genesis 32.xxv

"He fell into the darkness and I caught him.
His eyes were closed, he did not wish to see
A man embrace him, he being an angel.
As long as he kept his eyes shut his lips could sing
Against my skin, he was so new, his hair
Feathering at the nape, his chest and sides
Smooth, his legs and thighs, not a hint of down,
An aura merely, the face rapt with desire.
What colour were his eyes? He kept them closed,
Like Cupid, blind, and would not meet my eye.

"That was the wrestle I had with the angel.
It was not about naming. I witnessed him,
Each inch of him I touched and kissed and loved
But he, who took the worship from my fingers,
Who drained me of desire, who made me love,
Left, though I held him hard, left though I held him,
Eyes screwed tight shut, bolted down, he went
Out of my arms like vapour, like a sigh.

"They say we wrestled: he came down and challenged.
It is not so. I had been there already
Almost asleep, he fell into my arms
And how could I not love him? Let me say:
He was an angel but he had no wings;
He was light and luminous and left behind
A darkness and a blindness, I was blind
Because he did not look at me or name me.

Imagine that: my fingers on his face
Could not prise up his eyes. We lay there breathing
After a long night. That's when they found us
And tried the story out that we'd been wrestling,
He was an angel, I was Jacob. He changed my name.
I said it had been so and he said nothing.
He was away, trailing his shirt, he vanished.
I said it had been so, yes, he had named me.

"The place I called Peniel because I saw
God's face and lived, and lived to tell the story.
I did not see his eyes, though, just his face,"

And the sun rose upon him and he passed over.

Furniture for a Ballad

Mas, ¡ay Madre de piedad!,
que sobre la cruz le tienden,
para tomar la medida
por donde los clavos entren.
                Lope de Vega

The standing stone, the stricken tree,
The sheep among, who leave their wool,
Who crop and tup, and drop their lambs,
Into a storm, beneath a moon . . .

The rider on his foaming horse
At night, to ship, to tryst, to tomb,
Or to a battlefield to find
The long corpse of his broken lord . . .

And in Dunfermline, swilling wine
Another lord, who sneers and wipes
His signet hand across his jowl,
Calls for his whore, his harp, his hound . . .

The new moon rocks the old, old moon
In its bowed arms, as if a child;
The old moon fades into a bruise,
The new moon fattens on its pain.

And who is she there on the prow
Of castle, town, of manse or grange
Gazing in dread that it is death
She sees, her lover on the heath

Coming to her to breathe his last
Into her mouth, a kiss, a cough;
She hungers for him and that breath
He feeds her at a stanza's end,

So like a host upon the tongue
And in his side a gash, his feet
Holed, and his hands. Don't call him Christ.
Leave him unnamed and cradle him.

The borders, marches deep in furze,
The dripping rocks, the swelling moor,
The stricken tree, all see him pass
On his high steed. Is he the Word?

He rides away and leaves deep cloud,
A fleece of grace, the woman still
High on the prow, her arms awake
To catch him living, hold him dead.

He travels south, where he will climb
A higher cross than any here.
Though he passed here and everywhere,
He took his blood and bread away

To Palestine, where prophets said
He'd live and die and rise again.
Within the ballad death is death.
It cannot pray, it can't believe.

And yet it might go after him
Bear him back to stretch him here
Because of love, because of love,
The night, the maid, the sheep among:

A ballad cannot raise the dead.
It grieves and kills, it grieves again.
Let her in the blown midnight wait
Like a new moon imbibing pain.

Thus he will live and she expect
His visit and her ravishment,
His lips, the thunder of his pulse,
Her handsome womb his citadel . . .

Leave metaphysics to the Jews.
The crofter minds his wretched sheep,
The lord is rusting in the rain,
The woman stifles a fat yawn,

Goes in, sits down, he has not come.
She drinks a potion, sleeps and dreams,
The standing stone, the stricken tree,
Into a storm, beneath a moon . . .

We lose her as the night resigns
And so it is, the ballad's made
Out of such furniture as these,
The dripping fern, a daylight moon.

Between

The arrow thirled right through,
The feathers—white as it flew,
Red when it struck the tree—
Stayed like a grafted bough.

A bird perched on the end
Whetting its yellow beak,
Stuck in blood as in lime
Flapped, flailed. Another slain.

*

Buy metamorphosis from Rome:
A tree the cross, and wine the blood,
Bread the flesh, or gingerbread:
The truth is neither this nor that

But what's amid, whatever is
Between a tattered coat and age,
Between a lion and a king,
Leviathan and Lucifer,

A feathered arrow and a bird,
Quicklime and blood, a flapping wing
And life itself, a bow and love:
Call them two dots: the line between.

*

Language can never quite translate
The motion there or draw the line.
That's where the mystery abides:
The process, not the A or B,

The place where substance (alchemy!)
Transforms and cannot be turned back;
The wine is salty in the wound,
The loaf is baking on the cross.

It is not only Christ who's given
Such bold transitions, such regrets,
To hold him in our hands and mouths,
To swallow and ourselves become.

*

If we should find ourselves alone
Inside the cave of Proteus
Whether a woman or a man
The creature is, divine or brute,

It is the squeeze and punch and hug,
The gasp and grasp, the pinch and pull,
It is the kiss, the holding close,
And not the lover cowled in weed

Or what it was when you embraced
First in the half-light of the cave,
The water lapping at your thighs,
The smell of fish and excrement.

It's not the radiance finally
You hold; but rather, how you got
From it to him or her, to you,
Is where the mystery abides.

Not Yet

My father said he'd have to cut the tree down,
It was so high and broad at the top, and it leaned
In towards the house so that in wind it brushed
The roof slates, gables and the chimney stone
Leaving its marks there as if it intended to.

We said, don't cut it yet, because the tree was so full
Of big and little nests, of stippled fruit.
In spring and summer it spoke in a thousand voices,
The chicks upturned for love, the birds like fishes
Swimming among the boughs, and always talking.

And then a day came when the chicks woke up.
Love was all over, they tumbled from their nests
Into the air, ricocheted from a leaf, a branch,
Almost hit the ground, then found their wings
And soared up crying, brothers, sisters, crying.

Then the nests were vacant. Now we must cut the tree,
My father said. Again we begged, not yet,
Because with autumn the freckled fruit began
To turn to red, to gold, like glowing lamps
Fuelled with sweetness filtered from the soil

And scent that was musk and orange, peach and rose.
And when they dropped (they grew on the topmost branches,
Could not be picked, we took when it was offered)
We wiped them clean and sliced out the darkening bruise
Where they'd bounced on the yellow lawn, by then quite hard

With winter coming. The fruit were so much more than sweet,
Eve fell for such fruit and took Adam with her:
No serpent whispered, no god patrolled the garden.
Only my father. Again, not yet, we said, remembering
What winter had to do with our huge bent tree,

Once it had got the leaves off. We knew the hoar-frost
Tracery and the three-foot icicles
And how it simply was, the December moon
Lighted upon it and hung in its arms like a child.
Not yet, we said, not yet. And my father died,

And the tree swept the slates clean with its wings.
The birds were back and nesting, it was spring,
And nothing had altered much, not yet, not yet.

The Resurrection of the Body

. . . So will I melt into a bath to washe them in my bloode . . .
S. Robert Southwell S.J.

The cellar floor is swept. Women are weeping
Like shadows in torchlight, around the straw pallet they hover,
The soon-to-be-mourners, a dozen, discarding their shawls,
Unpinning their hair. It's so hot in the cellar of death.
Professional, they know what's to come:
She will shrug, shiver, jaw drop open, let go.

Led out of blinding daylight the Healer comes down.
He raises his hand and stills the scrum of women.
He comes down like a lamp into a cavern,
Gathering from sweltering noon light a cool glow.
He comes as if out of the desert sequinned with dew
And his gaze, austere, not unkind, goes through the women
Settling on the parched form stretched on the pallet,
Human, almost beyond pain, but not a child.
The man did say *child* but she is almost a woman,
Her delicate feet, long legs, the down at her crotch,
Flat belly, firm, the handsome small domes of her breasts
Panting, panting, not a child, though her father, grieving,
Insists, believing, a child. So he says to her, *child*.

She focuses her dark gaze on his amazing pallor,
Her fever like a bruise against him. She closes her lips
Reaching for a sheet, the rolled winding sheet, for cover
But he makes her calm, she understands, her lips now parted
Rapt, she holds her breath (she has breath to hold now).
She watches him, he bends down to her, to lift her up,
His shirt falls open, she sees where the wounds will be.

What does he feel when he gathers her hot and shivering
Off the pallet, hardly a weight, so smooth, and all
The smells upon her, faeces and stale sweat, the scent
Of her scalp, and her breath quite sweet, a surprise;
That hot smooth flesh, that shit and flowers, urine
And something else; and the haze of down on her arms
Up to the elbows, then the quite smooth darkness,
Substance of shadow, her flesh, so smooth, and the breathing
Not weary or fretful now in that limp body;

What does he feel, seeing his own white arm beneath her dark hair,
When he knows what he holds, and what it does to his legs,
To his groin, his bowels, to his rapid heart? He holds her
And out of his chest where she is pressed against him
Flows that unusual grace which is rooted in muscle,
Which comes from the marrow and lymph, which is divine,
The grace of a man whom love has turned into God,
The love of incarnate God whose flesh knows the name of his creature.
He holds her the way his mother will soon cradle him,
Passion giving life, or love; and then compassion.

And what does she feel? Who can know what she feels?
What you would feel, or I, pressed close to his chest,
To his cool skin, his smell of the dust of the road,
Of hearth fires, of wine, the touch of his hair, of bread . . .
What does she feel? She feels love, she feels his desire
Confusing her, desire but not need, he holds her
Tenderly, his lips to her shoulder and hair.

Out of the cellar he bears her into the air
Shedding her pestilence and the sun dissolves it.
A crowd has assembled. He walks among the crowd
With his light burden, they watch and withdraw, afraid,
Conjuror, they see the girl gaze in his eyes.

At the well he sets her down, she can stand on her own.
At the well she stands straight as a reed and Jesus bathes her,
First her hair, he pours water from a hollowed gourd,
Then her ears and eyes and lips, her face, her neck,
Her heart and hands, her back, her belly, her long thighs,
He washes her feet as if she were a child.
The fever has passed. She calls him *father, father*
Though the man who is her father stands beside him.
She calls him *father.* He wraps her in his own shirt.

Notes

"The Education of Henry Adams, Private Secretary"

When I came to read *The Education of Henry Adams* a few years ago I was especially taken with the chapters in which Henry's father was appointed American Minister in London, made his son his Private Secretary, and arrived at the Court of St James to find that the British had just recognized the Confederacy's belligerence. The time in Britain during the Civil War was one of great anguish and privation for young Henry; for the first three years it seemed the Union cause was lost and written off with a kind of hubristic glee by the Mother Country. I imagined him as affected by his absence from a series of defining traumas in his nation's history, feeling himself defined by his absence from them. The language of the poem draws from his actual text, phrases and portions of sentences being his, hence the semi-Cento form. Some of the phrases are also drawn from Faulkner, and some from Whitman. In order to avoid the elegiac tone and the iambic rhythm into which the voice tends to fall in reverie, I submitted to a severe syllabic rule, though not consistently rhyming. This was writing against the grain as much as possible. I was keen to make a poem that was American in the dignified way of Henry Adams, telling no more than the truth, but with luck no less, also. It feels a personal poem, but who that person is is hard to say.

"The Husband's Message"

From a letter to Greg Delanty, one of the editors of *The Word Exchange* (W.W. Norton, 2010): "I have tried to build the damaged manuscript into the translation, as part of the poem, hence the opening sound effects and the ending have an element of reconstruction which I believe, if the poem is a single poem, is called for, or if not called for, at least not poetically unjustifiable. So the wooden tablet speaks, as the Cross does in 'The Dream of the Rood,' and speaks for the husband, remote, now re-established in his fortunes far away. The conceit of the speaking tablet runs through the poem, so the tablet is in a sense the advocate, the go-between, a little attracted itself to the woman it speaks to on the husband's behalf. I have used commas within the hemistichs for grammatical and prosodic reasons, slight pauses, but no full stops, trusting the enjambment to compel the pause and counterpoint the syntax."

"In this Modest Style"

Ramón López Velarde fascinated me in my late teens and early twenties. I was urged to read him by Octavio Paz, who was aware of my love for Eliot and through Eliot for Laforgue. He wanted me to find resources in my own culture. (I was born and raised in Mexico.) There is common ground between the provincial poet of northern Mexico and Laforgue (born, after all, in Uruguay). There are tonal similarities, allusive narratives, wry and then wan romance, at home in the provinces, in the heat of the day and the cool of the evening. My mentor may have felt that Velarde would harden up my verse, for Velarde is all concentration, his slow and self-reflective pace is never monotonous but always alive and spoken. "His imagination," Octavio wrote, "did not lead him to flare up in blazes of artifice, but rather to go deeper into himself and to express with ever greater fidelity what he had to say." Fidelity is the deepest feeling for Velarde. He forged "a personal style" because he "had something personal to say." He lives a daily life and it is the meat and matter of his poetry because he lives it in a distinctive way. "We cannot write our way back to the poetry of Velarde because it constitutes our unique [Mexican] point of departure." Velarde is more formal, more buttoned up than Laforgue, his Catholicism severe, his libido certainly evident, but attenuated. In "Por este sobrio estilo," which I marked with three enthusiastic asterisks and a question mark when I first read it, I was beguiled by the intimacy of Velarde's speech, yet puzzled by the relationship the poem evokes. Was a precociously Oedipal child addressing his mother? But the flirtatiousness, the muted eroticism, and the relative youthfulness of the woman addressed, made it elusive to a modern reader. Velarde's "she," who becomes "you" in the second half of the poem, is in fact an idealised version of his relative Josefa de los Ríos, whom he met in his early teens and adored until she died. The first lost love, the impossible one, Fuensanta: if she was not to be his, she should be chaste until she withered, until her light went out. Velarde concentrates particularly on two images in this poem, the orange blossom and the star. They recur, they develop. The blossom breathes out its scent and the star rises in the sky; the blossom withers and the star sets. These two mark the times of the poem and its moods. It keeps a tense, even pace. The syntax repeats its patterns and builds, but the verse does not move towards song. It is spoken, intensely spoken. Its irregularities keep it within the world of colonial avenues, mother-of-pearl and ruffs, tablecloths and evening gardens. It is a world rich with restraint, touched with regret because the woman and the time are gone beyond recall. Not only has she perished; the Revolution has altered everything. One feels that in Velarde's heart there is a tension between his moral refusal to countenance physical intimacy and his palpable desire. The reading that the almost-lovers share: is that his poems? And the panegyrics that she must face: surely poems not unlike the one we are reading. Perhaps this is the very one to which she is responding, quiet and wry and teasing.

"Also, Poor Yorick," written for *The Reader*

In 1985 C.H. Sisson sent me his translation of Andreas Gryphius's "Gedancken über den Kirchhoff und Ruhestädte der Verstorbenen," first published in Breslau 1657. Gryphius's father was a Lutheran pastor, and the poet was born in Glogau, Silesia, a town recently ruined by fire. When he was two the Thirty Years' War began. His early sonnets, Sisson remarks, were about "this world of blood, pillage, fire, rape, famine." He was well educated and well travelled. He spent his last years back in Glogau as an official and there composed "Gedancken." I published it in full—fifty eight-line stanzas—as "Thoughts on the Churchyard and the Resting-places of the Dead" in *PN Review* 44 twenty-five years ago. This merciless poem could hardly be further from Gray's "Elegy." The poet imagines the final judgement and the opening of the graves. In the fifteenth stanza he writes:

> God help me. Coffins open wide,
> I see the bodies in them move.
> The army of the once alive
> Begins to exercise anew.
> I find myself surrounded by

A host death has deprived of power
A spectacle which forces showers
Of burning tears from my blank eyes.

He moves from this terror, through gloating at the fleshless, worm-rid-dled fate of his foes (less a mournful *ubi sunt* than a wry *ibi sunt*, reduced to burst skulls and disconnected bones), to a sense of his own mortality and, at last, to the promise of eternal life. Transfiguration in the poem is less real, less credible, than rank mortality and decomposition.

The Jacobean, baroque, grim wisdom of this poem is a sophisti-cation of the churchyard in Elsinore where Hamlet handles Yorick's skull. Gryphius's poem has stayed with me, both as a vision of mortality and as a teasing, unlikely promise of resurrection, a theme that fascinates the reluctant Anglican in me and the pagan lover of Ovid and the metamor-phoses of classical legend. One of my favourite poems by C.H. Sisson is "Metamorphoses": in it the classical stories are not driven out by Christ as in Milton's "On the Morning of Christ's Nativity," but redeemed. Sisson writes, "The metamorphosis of all/Or he was nothing but a child . . ."

Gryphius, Sisson and of course Shakespeare are behind "Also, Poor Yorick." Some readers will spot David Beckham, from the time of a World Cup injury, in ghostly form. Years ago I saw a Pre-Raphaelite painting of a swarm of saved souls in white gowns clouding up into the heavens. It was a huge, poor painting but a memorable vision that also informs the poem. The little jet of Latin is conventional: I first read the epitaph on a gravestone pavement in Toledo in my late teens: *Hic iacet pul-vis cinis nihil*, anonymous. There is a painting by a colonial Mexican artist in the gallery of the Viceregency in Mexico City showing Christ with a spear or arrow in his side upon which a phoenix perches. Sebastian is never far away. The arrival of Hamlet, too equivocal to believe, too self-engrossed, is not a Stoppard gesture. In the larger drama it is Yorick who shows the way and poor Hamlet who has the walk-on part.